KT-465-776

Track

Tony Ward

Heinemann

First published in Great Britain by Heinemann Publishers
(Oxford) Ltd
Halley Court, Jordan Hill, Oxford OX2 8EJ

MADRID ATHENS PARIS
FLORENCE PRAGUE WARSAW
PORTSMOUTH NH CHICAGO SAO PAULO
SINGAPORE TOKYO MELBOURNE AUCKLAND
IBADAN GABORONE JOHANNESBURG

Designed by VAP Group Ltd
Printed in the UK by Jarrold Printing, Norwich.

00 99 98 97 96
10 9 8 7 6 5 4 3 2 1

ISBN 0 431 05947 0

British Library Cataloguing in Publication Data

Ward, Tony
  Track. – (Olympic Library)
  I. Title II. Series
  796.2

Acknowledgements
The Publishers would like to thank the following for permission to reproduce photographs:
Allsport: p.8, 9, 15, 18, 20, 21, 23; Associated Sports Photography: p.5, 13, 14;
Colorsport: p.6, 7, 10, 11, 12, 16, 17, 19, 22, 26, 27; Hulton Deutsch Collection: p. 4, 24, 28;
Range/Bettmann/UPI: p.25, 29.

Cover photographs reproduced with permission of Allsport and Professional Sport.
Cover designed by Brigitte Willgoss.

Our thanks to Mr Robert Paul of the US Olympic Committee and Mr Paul Rowbotham for their comments in the
preparation of this book.

Olympic rings logo reproduced with the permission of the International Olympics Committee.

Every effort has been made to contact copyright holders of any material reproduced in this book.
Any omissions will be rectified in subsequent printings if notice is given to the Publisher.

Contents

Track at the Olympics

Athens 1896: Spyridon Louis, the winner of the marathon, passing the post.

Track events have always played a major part in the Olympic Games. For many years the ancient Games consisted of just one event, the stadium race. Later, other distances were added.

When a Frenchman, Baron Pierre de Coubertin, decided to make plans to revive the Olympic Games in the late part of the nineteenth century, athletics was becoming an important sport, especially in Britain. In those early days, meetings took place mostly at universities and schools.

The Olympics Start Again

The first modern Olympic Games, in 1896, included track events. They were held in a marble stadium in Athens which still stands today.

Only men took part, because such public exercises were considered unsuitable for women. The standard was not very high, and the performances in these first Olympics could easily be bettered by school athletes today.

The event that most people remember from these Olympics is the **marathon** race which was run from the village of Marathon to the stadium, a distance of around 42 km or 26 miles. The race was supposed to commemorate the original run of the Greek messenger, Pheidippides, who carried news of the Greek victory over the Persians in 490BC. The 1896 race was won by a Greek shepherd, Spyridon Louis, who gained his country's only victory. In Athens, the USA won nine **gold medals** in the track events and Australia won two.

Olympic Track Events

Men	Women
100 m	100 m
200 m	200 m
400 m	400 m
800 m	800 m
1500 m	1500 m
5000 m	5000 m
10 000 m	10 000 m
110 m hurdles	100 m hurdles
400 m hurdles	400 m hurdles
3000 m steeplechase	
4 × 100 m relay	4 × 100 m relay
4 × 400 m relay	4 × 400 m relay
marathon	marathon
20 km walk	10 km walk
50 km walk	

Different track events have come and gone over the years in the Olympic Games. At various times there has been a 60 metres race (1900 and 1904), a 3000 metres/3 mile team race (1908–1924), individual and team **cross-country**, 200 metres **hurdle races** and a variety of walk races. All of these have now been dropped as Olympic events.

Names to Remember

The most popular events of the Games over the years have been the 100 metres, the 1500 metres and the distance races. The Americans, with their powerful **sprinters**, have won more 100 metres titles, fifteen in all, than any other country. Great Britain has made a national speciality of the 800 metres and 1500 metres events, winning six of the 800 metres and five of the 1500 metres races.

The Finnish runners completely dominated the distance events between 1912 and 1936 and again, for a short time, in the 1970s. In modern times the names of Carl Lewis (USA), in the 100 metres, Sebastian Coe (Great Britain) in the 1500 metres and Lasse Viren (Finland) in the 5000 and 10 000 metres, have become identified with being among the greatest ever in their events.

Women have made their mark, too, with athletes such as Wilma Rudolph (USA), Florence Griffith-Joyner (USA) and Irene Szewinska (Poland) making a great impact upon Olympic track events.

Emil Zatopek of Czechoslovakia leading in a 10 000 metre race in 1955.

Olympic Year

It is every athlete's ambition to compete in the Olympic Games – to become an **Olympian**. At the beginning of the Olympic year the track stars, confident of their selection, focus on the Olympics themselves. For others who hope to make the team it is the Olympic **trials** that are the target.

Getting Nervous

Training varies from event to event and most of the hard work is done during the winter before the Games. Sprinters do power work such as weight training or pulling a heavy tyre along the track, as well as **endurance** work. Distance runners run up to 160 km (almost 100 miles) a week, often training twice a day. An athlete will sometimes even give up work to concentrate on preparation. Some distance runners will try high altitude training, while sprinters and jumpers may travel to warmer climates away from the unpredictable British winter. Others have to endure the cold, the wet and the wind. While most athletes follow a diet that is very similar to that of a non-competitor, many rely on vitamin supplements to assist them during hard training. No stone is left unturned to ensure that every athlete arrives at the national **trials** and the Olympic Games in the very best physical condition possible.

As the training intensifies, there is always the fear of injury. A severe injury could mean losing weeks of training and could even prevent an athlete from taking part in the Games. Treatment can be costly and time-consuming. In order to be ready for the big events, a competitor may be in a race against time to recover physically and be on **form**.

Athletes have to warm up and stretch thoroughly before each event.

Selection Time

Each country has a different selection system. The most harsh are the American trials where the first three competitors in just one official race are selected automatically for that event. A few world record holders or world champions have failed to be selected because of illness, injury or just lack of form on the day of the event trial. In 1948, the great American hurdler, Harrison Dillard, failed to make the team in his event, so he switched to the 100 metres, qualified and won the Olympic title in London!

In Britain, an athlete is chosen for the track team in a particular event by coming first in that event trial. The selectors then pick up to two other competitors, but they don't have to pick the next two fastest at the trial.

The strain of qualifying for the Olympic Games can be seen on the faces of the competitors at the trials. It is almost inevitable that in the run-up to the Games, something dramatic will happen somewhere – an athlete trips, falls or fails to finish. Then there is the strange problem of loss of form. In 1988, Sebastian Coe failed to win his trial and was not picked for the Games. Although he was the defending champion from the previous Olympics in Los Angeles in 1984, he failed to make it to Seoul.

For those who are selected the moment is very special and for a few days they can bask in the glory of being team members. For them it is a life's ambition achieved. They are going to the Olympics!

Sally Gunnell in a 400 metres hurdles trial at the 1992 Barcelona Olympics.

Off to the Games!

There is no greater thrill than being selected for your first Olympic Games. After the anxious waiting comes the congratulations of family, friends and club mates. In track events a runner usually hears of his or her selection through the media because teams are announced almost straight away. This is done not only to avoid 'leaks' but also to let those who have not been selected know as quickly as possible. Later a letter arrives confirming selection and for a few days the new team members enjoy the thrill of being an Olympian.

Ready to Go

For the Olympics, national team members always have a uniform blazer or special suit as well as the appropriate sporting gear. Often athletes travel to the National Olympic Association's headquarters to be kitted out.

In the few weeks leading up to the Games athletes will continue to compete. They need to fine-tune their performances to ensure that when they arrive at the Olympics they are at the **peak** of their **form**.

Carl Lewis (left) of the USA wins the 100 metres at the 1992 Zurich World Championships.

All athletes selected for the Olympics dream of standing on the victory rostrum.

Linford Christie, the fastest-ever European sprinter, is very good at reaching his best form at exactly the right time. He has won a **Grand slam** of 100 metres titles – Olympic, World, European and Commonwealth – by peaking at exactly the right moment.

In 1992 some of the men he beat in Barcelona ran their fastest times three or four months before. Linford's fastest time of the year was in the Olympic final.

Some of the well known competitors continue to race in the big meetings until just before the Games. Others go into a final period of training. All are anxious to avoid injury at this crucial time.

Take Off

Finally comes the moment when everything has been packed and the farewells have been said. The team, or part of it, gathers at the airport to fly to the Olympic city. For the majority of athletes, the most important thing will be taking part. But a few will be able to say to themselves, 'When I'm back I'll be the Olympic champion'.

Did you know?

The only track event on the Olympic programme that women do not compete in is the steeplechase. This could change at the Sydney Olympics in 2000 when a women's steeplechase may be scheduled for the first time.

At the Olympics!

In the days leading up to the 1992 Olympics, the big jets landing at Barcelona brought the teams who were to compete in the Games of the twenty-fifth **Olympiad**. The largest track teams came from the USA, Russia, Great Britain and Germany. For the first time in 24 years, Germany was competing as one country. One of the smallest teams came from Namibia, but it included one of the world's fastest sprinters, Frankie Fredericks.

Some of the world's greatest athletes came through the airport's customs hall to be greeted by the colourful flags and bunting that decorated the whole city. Carl Lewis, Linford Christie, Sally Gunnell and Gwen Torrance received the applause of spectators with smiles, and all four were to become Olympic champions.

Competitors were whisked away on special coaches to the **Olympic Village**, which was home for all the competitors and team officials. The Village was specially built on the Mediterranean seashore, with each team housed in blocks of flats. The sea breezes kept the athletes cool as they trained and relaxed in the lead-up to the track events.

Safe and Secure

Security is always strict in an Olympic Village. Competitors have to wear identity tags at all times. Some even sleep with them around their necks to make sure they don't get lost! Bags are electronically checked every time anyone enters the Village.

Athletes relaxing in the Olympic Village for the 1992 Games in Barcelona.

The enormous Olympic stadium built for the Barcelona Games.

Good food is essential for the athletes. As they come from all parts of the world, the chefs in the Village have to cater for many national tastes. Chefs from many countries are employed to prepare their own specialities.

In Barcelona, the tension mounted as the time for the **opening ceremony** got nearer. All the athletes were anxious to get on with their competition. To help them relax and keep their minds away from their races, competitors could travel into the city, using the Metro free of charge, to tour the famous buildings of Barcelona and stroll along the picturesque streets. However, seeing other competitors in their events would soon switch their minds back to the task in hand.

In the days immediately before the start of the track events, most of the major teams held their own team meetings. Details of the competitions were given by the team manager and the athletes collected their numbers and received details of transport to and from the stadium.

Once they had collected their competition numbers the athletes knew that the serious business was just around the corner. For them the Olympics were about to begin.

Did you know?

The winner of the 1932 women's 100 metres event, Stanislawa Walasiewicz, later emigrated to the USA where she changed her name to Stella Walsh. She was killed during a robbery in 1980 and the autopsy revealed her to be part man and part woman.

11

In Action

After the athletes arrive at the **Olympic Stadium**, they are all treated exactly the same. They have to follow the same procedures, and obey the same rules. The slowest athlete and the world record holder report at the same time, walk together to the stadium from the warm-up track and wait in the same room. There is no special treatment for the champions or the famous.

Final Preparations

At the stadium, the athletes prepare for their races on the warm-up track. The **physiotherapists**, whatever the hour, give massages on their couches in tents around the track. Each athlete has their own warm-up routine.

This usually includes some jogging, some exercises and some striding. It is timed to finish just before the athletes are called up to walk to the main stadium, already crowded with spectators.

The track athletes are summoned in two languages over a loud-speaker system. 'Competitors in heat one report now,' a steward will say. Each athlete knows their **heat** and will report to the stewards when called.

The tension amongst the competitors grows. Even the very great athletes need a certain amount of pre-event 'nerves' for a good performance. As the time comes nearer the nerves increase but the best athletes learn to control them and use the tension positively.

Linford Christie (second left) running in an early heat of the 100 metres in the 1992 Games.

Runners prepare for their event, with the officials standing by.

The runners step out into the stadium and get ready to compete. They adjust their **starting blocks**, and practise a few starts. When everyone is ready the starter will blow a whistle, the runners will take off their warm-up suits and get into their lane.

Each runner wears a number both on the sides of the vest and on the sides of the shorts to assist the **photo-finish camera**. The supporters from the runners' countries are there to cheer and wave flags to encourage them.

There are usually about 80 athletes in the opening heats of the 100 metres. This is reduced to only 32 after the second round heats later on the first day.

At Barcelona, Christie and Burrell both qualified easily, as did the other favourites. None of them were running at full speed. The really serious sprinting was saved for the next day.

At Barcelona, even though they knew they would qualify easily from the first round, Leroy Burrell and Linford Christie took no chances with their preparation. When their heats were called they walked with a steward and their rivals to the waiting room under the stadium. They knew that the fastest sprinters were kept apart by the draw and wouldn't meet in the first round.

For most competitors the first round can be a make or break time. They all are anxious to qualify for the next round so they can travel home with some pride, even if they do not win. To do this they must finish in the first three or four or qualify as a **fastest loser**.

Behind the Scenes

Track judges marching to their positions.

At any Olympic Games there are thousands of people who assist with the organizing and officiating, almost all of them unpaid volunteers.

In athletics there are technical officials, who judge the events. There are also stewards who control the movement of the runners and the officials to and from the events. They organize the victory ceremonies, and run the **doping control**. With each team there are managers, coaches, doctors and physiotherapists, all of whom are there to help the members of their team.

Judges, Starters and Stewards

Despite the arrival of electronic judging equipment, judges are still required. On the track they may help confirm the results of the photo-finish cameras and electronic timings.

Another very important official is the starter. It is the starter's job to make sure that races begin fairly with no-one gaining an advantage by starting early. A false start is sometimes called a **flyer**. The starting pistol used by the starter is electronically linked to the automatic timing.

There may also be stewards all around the Olympic Stadium. They guide the athletes from the warm-up track to the stadium, and help with security. Some stewards are attached to the teams, and help the team managers with their job. Many of the stewards are young men and women on summer vacation from schools and universities.

Team Staff Members

Team managers play an important part within the track teams. His or her job is to make sure that everything runs smoothly. The team manager has to see that the Olympic Village is comfortable for the runners, and that the food they want is available. In the stadium the team manager is there at the finish of races to congratulate athletes if they win or support them if they lose. The team manager is the most important official attached to any team.

Team coaches do not do much coaching at an Olympic Games. It's much too late for that! They give technical support, time training runs and calm nerves on the warm-up track. It is their responsibility to make sure that the runners arrive on time for their races.

Some of the most overworked people at any Olympic Games are the physiotherapists with the teams. Their days often begin at around dawn and go on to well past midnight. They massage tired muscles, and treat injuries.

Linford Christie with his coach, Ron Roddan.

Fulfilling the Dream

The semi-finals and final of the men's 100 metres are usually run on the second day of athletics at the Olympic Games. In the afternoon, the sixteen fastest men from the heats arrive for the semi-finals at the Olympic stadium. Eight men, four from each race, go forward to the final in the evening.

Barcelona Gold 1992

This was the position in which the British sprinter Linford Christie found himself at the Barcelona Olympic Games. He had to get through the semi-finals so he could go for gold in the evening. On the warm-up track Christie was as calm as usual. He was building up to the final. He would run only as fast as necessary to qualify. In the first semi-final against the American, Leroy Burrell, Burrell won in 9.97 seconds. Christie came next with 10.00 seconds. The second semi-final was won in a time of 10.07 seconds. These races made Burrell the favourite to win Olympic gold.

The stadium was totally packed for the 100 metres final. Everyone wanted to see who would be called the 'Fastest Man on Earth'. In Britain twelve million people watched the race on television.

There was a buzz of excitement as the runners began their preparations – setting their starting blocks, practising a few starts and, above all, concentrating. Losing concentration in an Olympic sprint race can lose a runner the gold medal.

Linford Christie winning the 100 metres in Barcelona in 1992.

Gail Devers on the victory rostrum after winning the gold medal in the women's 100 metres, Barcelona.

The starter blew the whistle. Christie stood like a statue staring down the track, almost as if he was in a trance. The other runners jumped about or ran on the spot, trying to calm their nerves. The stadium fell silent as the runners took their marks. They held a steady position and then Burrell made a false start. Knowing that a second false start would mean **disqualification**, Burrell lost his nerve and was too slow off the mark when the race started.

The Canadian Bruny Surin took the lead at the start but was soon overtaken by Christie who sprinted home to win in a time of 9.96 seconds. Frankie Fredericks of Namibia in second place won his country's first ever Olympic medal, and Dennis Mitchell of the USA was third.

A Moment of Glory

As he crossed the finish line the thunderous roar of the crowd flowed over Linford Christie. Photographers and TV cameras surrounded him. After shaking hands with his opponents he set out on a lap of honour, blowing kisses to the crowd. The Union Jacks, the Stars and Stripes and flags of all kinds waved in appreciation. It was one of the greatest moments of his life.

Making the Commitment

Many great track champions have been inspired by the achievements of the stars of their childhood and youth. Britain's Roger Bannister went to Wembley Stadium in London to see the 1948 Olympic Games. He was inspired by this occasion and went on to become the world's first four-minute mile runner – he also finished fourth in the 1952 Olympic Games 1500 metres. When Frank Shorter won the Olympic Marathon in Munich in 1972 he inspired millions of Americans to take up running for sport and fitness. In 1936, Jesse Owens' skill in winning four medals at the Berlin Olympics inspired generations of African-American athletes. Joan Benoit, USA, won the first women's Olympic Marathon in Los Angeles in 1984 and made women's long-distance running an accepted activity.

The Starting Point

Most champions begin their running at school and then find they are faster or can run for longer than their classmates. The great Trinidadian sprinter Emmanuel McDonald Bailey found out he was fast when his father couldn't catch up to punish him!

Brandon Rock wins the 800 metres at the NCAA championships in the USA.

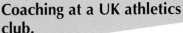
Coaching at a UK athletics club.

Since school sports is the starting point for an athletics career, the physical education teacher is the earliest coach. In Great Britain, the next rung of the ladder is the athletics club. In the USA, the high school and college athletics programmes provide the training ground for champions with their fierce competitions. Well-paid professional coaches are available at all levels in America. In Britain the vast majority of the coaches are volunteers who work for no money.

Enjoy Your Running

Ask any great champion what is important for a young runner at the beginning of a career and they will almost always say, 'Enjoy it'. Young athletes, no matter how good they may be at one particular event, should try others. Steve Ovett, the 1980 Olympic 800 metres champion, was a very good long jumper at school. So was Sally Gunnell, who also tried the heptathlon before she specialized in hurdles. The javelin thrower Steve Backley's father was a cross-country runner so, for a period of time, Steve tried that event as well!

If an athlete is very young when he or she is recognized as being very good, the training should be less intense. Many potential Olympic runners have been driven away from the sport by the drudgery and boredom of hard training over too many years. It is important that a runner finds an understanding coach who knows how to help young athletes. To a serious runner, a coach is like a teacher, parent and best friend rolled into one.

Some athletes show such real talent at a young age that it is obvious to everyone around them that they will become great one day. In 1966, Jim Ryan, the American miler, achieved a time of 3 minutes 51.3 seconds at age nineteen. When Mary Rand, the great British all-rounder, was a student at Millfield School, her coach was watching her one day and then said, 'Do you want to go to the Olympic Games?'. She was just fourteen. In 1964, at the age of 24, she became an Olympic champion.

Making the Grade

No athlete has appeared in an Olympic Games without making a serious **commitment** to their sport. For track athletes this means hour upon hour of running training, through cold and wet winters and hot summers on all sorts of terrain. There is no substitute for hard work when you dream of Olympic gold!

Training, Training and More Training

Training is a steady progression, gradually increasing in intensity. No two runners train in exactly the same way. The most successful athletes adapt training ideas and patterns to suit themselves.

Many young runners overdo the hard slog of training. Sometimes they even become bored or burnt out and retire from the sport long before their prime.

Getting to the top also means a steady progression through more and more difficult levels of competition. From schools level competition, talented runners move to junior championship level. Most countries and continents hold junior championships. In the USA, as well as the national meetings there is also a **Pan-American** meeting. In Europe the most important meeting is the European Junior Championships. In all cases these are only for athletes under twenty years of age and are held every two years.

At the World Junior Championships in Seoul in 1992, Ato Bolden of Trinidad (centre) wins his second gold medal in the 200 metres.

Frank Bussman winning the 110 metres hurdles at the 1994 World Junior Championships in Lisbon.

Junior Champions

The highest ambition for a junior runner is to take part in the World Junior Championships, also held every two years. It is here that junior runners have a chance to compare themselves with runners from the rest of the world. Winning times in performances at these championships often compare very well with the seniors' times. In 1992, at the World Junior Championships in Seoul, Korea, the winning time for the women's 3000 metres was almost identical to that run by the gold medallist at the Barcelona Olympics!

Often the most difficult time in a runner's career comes when the change is made from competing at junior level to competing against older, more experienced and faster athletes. Many of the junior champions fail to make the grade as seniors and fade away from the sport. Patience and belief in one's ability at this point are very important. Gradually the really talented and dedicated youngsters equal and then start to beat the seniors. Then the Olympic dream begins to look like a possibility.

Drugs = Cheating!

Young runners can be exposed to pressure to use drugs or **banned substances** to improve their performance. There is a battle against drugs in track athletics just as there is in other sports. Taking drugs to improve performance is cheating and is definitely bad for the health. A German athlete in the 1980s, Birgit Dressel, died from the effects of the many drugs she was taking. The great drug sensation of the Seoul Olympics was the **disqualification** and banning of the winner of the 100 metres, Ben Johnson of Canada, for taking drugs. He let down his team-mates, family, friends and even his country through his cheating.

Getting to the Top

Each year the athletics calendar brings major competitions, especially for those in Europe. There is a cycle of events leading to the Olympics: World Championships – European Championships – Commonwealth Games – World Championships – Olympic Games. American athletes can take part in the Pan-American Championships between the World Championships. There is also the World Cup competition every four years and the European Cup every year.

Running for Money

There are also **Grand Prix meetings** around the world. Here the runners can be paid appearance money, and the better the runner the more appearance money they can demand.

The most important Grand Prix meetings are at Oslo, Zurich, Nice and Brussels. At the end of the season there is the Grand Prix final. The overall winner can receive at least $100 000 in prize money. At the beginning of each year the best athletes sit down with the coaches and **agents** or managers and plan their programme. Almost always the main aim is to compete in the big championships. Many runners are also looking one or two years ahead to the Olympic Games.

At the major athletics championships the procedures and programme are almost always the same. **Qualifying times** are important. These are set by the international body and runners try to reach them early in the season to avoid a panic at the end.

Roger Black sprints to victory in the 1990 European Championships.

Leroy Burrell sets a 100 metres world record (9.90 seconds) at the US championships in 1991.

Success and Fame

Success at the European, Pan-American or World Championships can make an enormous difference to a runner, both financially and in terms of fame. Linford Christie entered 1986 as only one of half a dozen good British sprinters. He went into 1987 as a challenger for the world title. Becoming European champion in Stuttgart made that difference.

The time between victory in the World Championships and the next Olympic Games can be the downfall of some runners. Once the World Championships in Tokyo in 1991 were over, runners' thoughts turned almost immediately to the Barcelona Olympics in 1992.

However, there were twelve months in between in which injury and loss of **form** just waited to strike! Of all the 1991 individual World champions from Tokyo, only two, Marie-Jose Perec (400 metres) and Hassiba Boulmerka (1500 metres) went on to win a year later in Barcelona.

Did you know?

Really talented runners sometimes have to decide to give up their careers or education to become full-time athletes. This can be a very difficult decision to make. All it takes is a loss of form or an injury and the runner may end up with no future in athletics, no job and no further education.

Looking Back

The Early Days

The first group of runners really to make an impression at the Olympic Games were the 'Flying Finns' as they came to be known. The first Finn was Hannes Kohlemainen who won both the 5000 metres and 10 000 metres at the 1912 Games in Stockholm. Finnish runners then won every 5000 and 10 000 metres title from 1912 to 1936, except in 1932 when other runners won the gold medals. The most famous of these Finnish runners was Paavo Nurmi who, at the 1924 Olympic Games in Paris, won both the 5000 and 10 000 metres and the cross-country race. He ran lap after lap at the same pace, often carrying a stop watch in his hand to check his times.

The USA has dominated the sprint events, winning eight out of ten 100 metres titles. Their most famous champion was the black sprinter Jesse Owens who won four gold medals in 1936 at the Olympic Games in Berlin.

It was also at the Berlin Olympics that Great Britain had one of its most famous victories in the 4 × 400 metres **relay**. Since 1912 when this event entered the Olympics programme the Americans had won all but one of the contests. However, in 1936 Great Britain had a world-class team. In a thrilling race, the Americans were beaten by two seconds.

Women Runners

Women entered the running events in 1928 with the 100 and 800 metres. The first champion was Betty Robinson of the USA. In the 800 metres, many women collapsed after they had finished and the officials, all men, considered such goings on very 'unladylike'! This event for women did not return to the Olympics programme until 1964.

The only individual track events for women at the 1932 Olympics in Los Angeles were the 100 metres and 80 metres hurdles. The hurdles race was won by Mildred 'Babe' Didrikson of the USA, one of the greatest all-round sportswomen the world has ever seen.

War and Games

The 1940 Olympic Games were due to be staged in Tokyo but World War 2 prevented them from being held. Many world-class runners lost their chance to run for their country and win Olympic medals. One of the most famous was the German Rudolf Harbig, who was then the world-record holder for the 400 and 800 metres. He was killed on the Russian front fighting for Germany during the war.

In More Modern Times

The first great Olympic hero on the track after World War 2 was the Czechoslovakian, Emil Zatopek. He won the 10 000 metres in London in 1948 but it was in Helsinki, four years later, that he became a running legend. He won both the 5000 and 10 000 metres and on the last day he entered the marathon. After thirteen miles, as they ran along together, he asked the favourite, Englishman Jim Peters, if the pace was fast enough. Peters, feeling tired, gasped a reply. Zatopek just nodded and then sped away to win!

National Specialities

The American sprinters dominated the first six Olympic 100 metres held after the war. The greatest of them all was Bob Hayes, who won in Tokyo in 1964 by the greatest margin to date. His time of 10.06 seconds would still be considered world-class even today.

In 1972 the Finnish runners made a great return to the Olympics. Lasse Viren won the distance double of the 5000 and 10 000 metres races and repeated this feat in 1976. He is the only runner ever to do this.

Florence Griffith-Joyner (USA) wins the 100 metres gold medal at the 1988 Seoul Olympics.

Four Medals!

The only Olympic athlete to win medals in four different individual events is the Pole, Irene Szewinska. She won silver in the long jump in 1964, 100 metres bronze in 1968, gold in the 200 metres in 1968 and gold in the 400 metres in 1976. She broke the record of the famous Dutch athlete Fanny Blankers-Koen, who won the 100 metres and 200 metres and the hurdles in 1948.

Two great American sprinters emerged in the 1980s. In 1984 Carl Lewis won four athletics gold medals in Los Angeles. He repeated his 100 metres win in Seoul in 1988 in the famous race where Ben Johnson was disqualified for drug abuse.

In 1988, the current women's world record holder, Florence Griffith-Joyner (nicknamed Flo Jo), won both the sprint races, setting a new world record time of 21.54 seconds in the 200 metres. Many male sprinters at the time who had similar performance times refused to believe that a woman could run as fast as they could!

The Finnish 1500 metres runner, Paako Vassala, also won in 1972. Since that time the distance running events have been totally dominated by athletes from Kenya and Ethiopia.

In 1972 the German Democratic Republic (GDR) entered the Olympics as a separate country from Western Germany. Immediately they began to dominate the women's events, competing with the USSR for medals. Their greatest track runners were Marita Koch (400 metres) and Renate Stecher, who achieved a sprint double (100 metres and 200 metres) in 1972. After the collapse of the Communist regimes in eastern Europe and the USSR and the reunifying of Germany, reports came out of drug abuse by some GDR athletes.

Did you know?

On the day that Emil Zatopek won the 5000 metres in Helsinki in 1952, his wife, Dana, won the women's javelin.

Track Chat

The youngest ever male track competitor in the modern Olympic Games is Farhad Navab of Iran, who was only 16 years, 61 days old when he competed in the 100 metres in Munich in 1972. Heather Gooding of Barbados, the youngest woman, was only 14 years, 104 days when she also competed at Munich 800 metres. In 1968, Esther Stroy of the USA ran the 400 metres in Mexico City aged 15 years, 65 days.

The oldest known male athlete ever to compete in the Olympic track events is Percival Wyer of Canada. He ran the marathon at the 1936 Games in Berlin when he was 52 years, 199 days old. The oldest woman competitor is Lourdes Klitzkie of Guam who was 48 years, 234 days old when she ran the 100 metres in Seoul in 1988.

Ralph Metcalfe of the USA (left) winning the silver medal in the 100 metres at the 1936 Berlin Games.

Second oldest woman is Joyce Smith of Great Britain who ran in the first ever women's marathon in 1984 when she was 46 years, 284 days old. Her team mate in the race was Priscilla Welch who was only 39 years 256 days old! In fact, that first women's marathon contained four of the ten oldest women ever to compete in Olympic athletics!

Elizabeth Robinson of the USA was the first ever woman's Olympic champion. She won gold in the 100 metres in 1928 when she was just 16 years, 343 days old. The oldest woman track gold medallist was Maricica Puica of Romania, who won the 3000 metres in Los Angeles in 1984. She was not expected to win, but the favourite, Mary Decker (USA), crashed out after she collided with the South-African-born Zola Budd who was running for Great Britain.

Paavo Nurmi of Finland has won twelve Olympic medals, the most by any competitor. Of the twelve, nine are gold medals! Carl Lewis of the USA has won eight Olympic medals, seven of them gold.

Irene Szewinska of Poland is the only track athlete to compete at five Olympic Games. She ran in all the Games from 1964 to 1980, a span of sixteen years.

There have been some very unlucky losers in Olympic track events. The American hurdler, Jack Davis, came second in two Olympics, in 1956 and 1960.

In 1932, the American sprinter Ralph Metcalfe equalled the then world record of 10.3 seconds but lost to Eddie Tolan who was even faster. Four years later Metcalfe again won the silver, coming second to Jesse Owens. The great Jamaican runner Herb McKenley has three individual silver medals, two at 400 metres and one at 100 metres, won in two Olympics in 1948 and 1952. He also has an Olympic gold medal which he won in the 4 × 400 metres relay in Helsinki in 1952! The Canadian Phil Edwards wasn't so lucky. He won five bronze medals in three Olympics from 1928 to 1936, three in the 800 metres and two in the 4 × 400 metres relay.

Glossary

agents people who negotiate appearance fees with meeting promoters on behalf of athletes

banned substances drugs on the banned list of the International Olympic Committee (IOC)

bronze medal prize awarded to those athletes who finish third in Olympic events

commitment dedication to preparing for an event

cross-country races run over hilly, grass terrain

disqualification what happens when an athlete breaks a rule

doping control a room at the stadium where athletes are drug tested after races

endurance stamina

fastest losers athletes who qualify for the next round of a track event by clocking the next fastest times after the heat winners and placers

flyer another name for a false start

form current standard

four-minute mile a mile race run in a time under four minutes

gold medal prize awarded to the winner of Olympic events

Grand Prix meetings the best meetings in the world which are given top status by the IAAF, the world governing body. There are Grand Prix 1 and Grand Prix 2 meetings

Grand slam holding Commonwealth, European, World and Olympic titles at the same time

heat preliminary round of a track competition

hurdle races races at 100 metres and 400 metres for women and 110 metres and 400 metres for men with ten flights of hurdles to jump in each race

IAAF International Amateur Athletic Federation

Marathon a road race over 42.1 km or 26 miles 385 yards

NOC National Olympic Committee, the single, all-powerful, IOC-recognized Olympic organization in each country.

Olympiad four year period between Olympic Games, the basic Greek method of measuring the passing of time; sometimes used to describe the Games themselves

Olympian an athlete who has competed in the Olympic Games

Olympic stadium a track and grandstand where the opening ceremony and track and field events take place

Olympic Village the specially built accommodation that houses all the teams at an Olympic Games

opening ceremony a special event on the opening day when the competing teams parade, the Olympic flag is raised and one athlete takes the Olympic oath on behalf of all the competitors

Pan-American event involving athletes from all over North, Central and South America

peak at one's best form

photo-finish camera a camera used to record electronically the finish of races

physiotherapist a trained man or woman who treats injuries

qualifying times the time required to compete in a track event at the Olympic Games

relays races which involve teams of four competing over given distances. Olympic relays are run over 4×100 and 4×400 metres for both men and women.

sprinters those athletes who run distances between 100 metres and 400 metres where speed is the most important factor

silver medal awarded to athletes finishing second in Olympic events

starter This is the official who has the responsibility of ensuring a fair start to a race

starting block a wedge-shaped object used to hold the foot or feet at a heel-up angle while a racer is in the start position. It assists athletes in driving forward from a crouch position

team coach one of the squad of national coaches, each specializing in certain events, who accompanies a team to the Olympics

team doctor a doctor who specializes in sports medicine and accompanies a team to the Olympics

team manager the person with administrative responsibility for the welfare of a team at the Olympic Games

team race races where team members score points according to their finishing position. Usually the team with the lowest number of points is the winner

training special routines followed by an athlete to bring about a better performance

trials athletics meetings from which selections for the Olympic Games are made

warm-up track a running track which may be adjacent to the Olympic Stadium where the athletes prepare for their competitions

Index

Numbers in plain type (19) refer to the text. Numbers in italic type (*16*) refer to captions.